Practical
Pasta Sauces

p^3

This is a P³ Book
First published in 2003

P³
Queen Street House
4 Queen Street
Bath BA1 1HE, UK

ISBN: 1-40540-936-3

Printed in China

NOTE

Cup measurements in this book are for American cups.
This book also uses imperial and metric measurements. Follow the same units
of measurement throughout; do not mix imperial and metric.
All spoon measurements are level: teaspoons are assumed to be 5 ml, and
tablespoons are assumed to be 15 ml. Unless otherwise stated,
milk is assumed to be whole milk, eggs and individual vegetables such as potatoes
are medium, and pepper is freshly ground black pepper.

The nutritional information provided for each recipe is per serving or per person.
Optional ingredients, variations, or serving suggestions have
not been included in the calculations. The times given for each recipe are an approximate
guide only because the preparation times may differ according to the techniques used by
different people and the cooking times may vary as a result of the type of oven used.

Recipes using raw or very lightly cooked eggs should be
avoided by infants, the elderly, pregnant women, convalescents,
and anyone suffering from an illness.

Contents

Introduction

Creative cooks will enjoy partnering their favorite sauces with a variety of pastas. Although there are classic combinations, such as Spaghetti Bolognese (see page 26) and Spaghetti Carbonara (see page 28), there are no rules, just guidelines, which are largely a matter of practicality, appearance, and taste. When you have tried the delicious sauce recipes featured in this book, you might like to try exciting new combinations of pastas and sauces. Long ribbons and round pasta give tomato-based and oil-based sauces something to cling to, while shaped pastas and hollow tubes are ideal for trapping chunkier sauces in their crevices.

Pasta shapes

Here are the main pasta shapes you are likely to find in your local store or delicatessen:

Anelli, anellini, anelletti small rings used for soup
Bavette, bavettini thin, oval tubes
Bigoli whole-wheat pasta from the Veneto
Bozzoli deeply-ridged, cocoonlike shapes
Brichetti "small bricks"
Bucatini long, medium-thick tubes
Cappelletti wide-brimmed hat shapes
Capelli d'Angelo, angel's hair pasta, thinner than capellini
Capellini fine strands of ribbon pasta
Casareccia short, curled lengths of pasta from Sicily, twisted at one end
Cavatappi short, thick corkscrew shapes
Chifferi, chifferini, chifferotti small, curved tubes
Conchiglie ridged shells
Conchigliette little shells used for soup
Corallini small rings

Cornetti ridged shells
Cravatte, cravattini bows
Creste di gallo "cock's comb," curved shapes
Dischi volante "flying saucers"
Ditali, ditalini "little thimbles," short tubes
Eliche loose, spiral shapes
Elicoidali short, ridge tubes
Farfalle bows

Fedeli, fedelini fine tubes twisted into skeins
Festonati short lengths, like festoons
Fettuccine narrow ribbon pasta
Fiochette, fiochelli small bows
Frezine broad, flat ribbons
Fusilli spindles or short spirals
Fusilli bucati thin spirals, like springs
Gemelli "twins," two pieces wrapped together
Gramigna "grass" or "weed," look like sprouting seeds; from Emilia Romagna
Lasagna flat, rectangular sheets
Linguine long, flat ribbons
Lumache smooth, snaillike shells
Lumachine U-shaped flat pasta
Macaroni, maccheroni long- or short-cut tubes, may be ridged or elbow-shaped
Maltagliati triangular
Orecchiette ear-shaped
Orzi tiny, ricelike grains
Pappardelle widest ribbons, straight with saw-tooth edges
Pearlini tiny disks
Penne "quills", short, thick tubes with diagonally cut ends
Pipe Rigate ridged, curved pipe shapes
Rigatoni thick, ridged tubes
Rotelle wheels
Ruote wheels

Semini seed shapes
Spaghetti fine, medium, and thick rods
Spirale two rods twisted into spirals
Strozzapreti "priest strangler," double-twisted strands
Tagliarini flat ribbons, thinner than tagliatelle
Tagliatelle broad, flat ribbons
Tortiglione thin, twisted tubes
Vermicelli fine, slender strands usually twisted into skeins
Ziti tagliati short, thick tubes

Basic pasta sauces

Béchamel, tomato, and cheese sauces add creamy richness or moisture to baked dishes. They are also easy to make. The sauces featured here are very versatile and you can ring the changes by adding other ingredients.

Béchamel sauce

1¼ cups milk
2 bay leaves
3 cloves
1 small onion
1¾ oz/50 g butter
6 tbsp all-purpose flour
1¼ cups light cream
pinch of freshly grated nutmeg
salt and pepper

1 Pour the milk into a small pan and add the bay leaves. Press the cloves into the onion, add to the pan, and bring the milk to a boil. Remove from the heat and set aside to cool.

2 Strain the milk into a pitcher. Rinse the pan. Melt the butter in the pan over medium heat and stir in the flour. Stir for 1 minute. Gradually stir in the milk. Cook the sauce, stirring, for 3 minutes. Add the cream and bring to a boil.

3 Remove the pan from the heat and season the sauce to taste with nutmeg, salt, and pepper.

Basic tomato sauce

2 tbsp olive oil
1 small onion, chopped
1 garlic clove, chopped
14 oz/400 g canned chopped tomatoes
2 tbsp chopped fresh parsley
1 tbsp chopped fresh oregano
2 bay leaves
2 tbsp tomato paste
1 tsp sugar
salt and pepper

1 Heat the oil over medium heat and cook the onion, until translucent. Add the garlic and cook for 1 minute. Stir in the remaining ingredients and season to taste.

2 Bring to a boil, lower the heat, and simmer for 15-20 minutes, or until reduced by half. Adjust the seasoning and remove and discard the bay leaves.

Cheese sauce

1 oz/25 g butter
1 tbsp all-purpose flour
1 cup milk
2 tbsp light cream
pinch of freshly grated nutmeg
1¾ oz/50 g grated sharp colby cheese
1 tbsp grated Parmesan cheese
salt and pepper

1 Melt the butter over medium heat. Stir in the flour and cook, stirring, for 1 minute. Stir in the milk, cream, and nutmeg. Season. Lower the heat; simmer for 5 minutes.

2 Remove from the heat and stir in the colby and Parmesan cheeses until melted. Serve.

KEY	
	Simplicity level 1–3 (1 easiest, 3 slightly harder)
	Preparation time
	Cooking time

Spicy Tomato Sauce

This deliciously fresh and slightly spicy tomato sauce is excellent with pasta and makes a satisfying lunch or light supper.

NUTRITIONAL INFORMATION

Calories	306	Sugars	.........7g
Protein	.........8g	Fat	..........12g
Carbohydrate	...45g	Saturates	.......7g

🐷 🐷 🐷

 15 mins   🕐 35 mins

SERVES 4

I N G R E D I E N T S

S A U C E

3 tbsp butter

1 onion, finely chopped

1 garlic clove, minced

2 small red chiles, seeded and diced

1 lb/450 g fresh tomatoes, skinned, seeded, and diced

¾ cup vegetable bouillon

2 tbsp tomato paste

1 tsp sugar

salt and pepper

P A S T A

1 lb 8 oz/675 g fresh green and white tagliatelle, or 12 oz/350 g dried pasta

1 Melt the butter in a large pan. Add the onion and garlic and cook for 3–4 minutes, or until soft.

2 Add the chiles and continue cooking for another 2 minutes.

3 Add the tomatoes and bouillon, then lower the heat and let simmer, stirring occasionally, for 10 minutes.

4 Pour the sauce into a food processor and blend for 1 minute, or until smooth. Alternatively, push the sauce through a strainer.

5 Return the sauce to the pan and add the tomato paste, sugar, and salt and pepper to taste. Gently reheat over low heat, until piping hot.

6 Cook the tagliatelle in a pan of boiling water according to the instructions on the package, or until it is cooked but still firm to the bite. Drain the tagliatelle and transfer to serving plates. Serve immediately with the tomato sauce.

VARIATION

Try using a different shape of pasta, such as penne, for this recipe, then put it in an ovenproof dish, top with some grated cheese, and bake for a warming winter feast.

Basil & Pine Nut Pesto

This pesto is delicious stirred into pasta, soups, and salad dressings. You can buy it ready-made, but making your own gives a concentrated flavor.

NUTRITIONAL INFORMATION

Calories	321	Sugars	. . . . .1g
Protein	. . . . .11g	Fat	. . . . .17g
Carbohydrate	. . .32g	Saturates	. . . . . . .4g

 15 mins   10 mins

SERVES 4

I N G R E D I E N T S

P E S T O

about 40 fresh basil leaves

3 garlic cloves, crushed

¼ cup pine kernels

½ cup Parmesan cheese, finely grated

2–3 tbsp extra-virgin olive oil

salt and pepper

P A S T A

1 lb 8 oz/675 g fresh pasta or 12 oz/350 g
  dried pasta

1 Rinse the basil leaves and pat them dry with paper towels.

2 Put the basil leaves, garlic, pine kernels, and grated Parmesan into a food processor, and blend for about 30 seconds, or until smooth. Alternatively, pound ingredients by hand, using a mortar and pestle.

3 If you are using a food processor, keep the motor running and slowly add the olive oil. Alternatively, add the oil drop by drop while stirring briskly. Season with salt and pepper to taste.

4 Cook the pasta in a pan of boiling water, allowing 3–4 minutes for fresh pasta or 8–10 minutes for dried, or until cooked through but still firm to the bite. Drain the pasta thoroughly in a colander.

5 Transfer the pasta to a serving plate and serve with the pesto. Toss to mix well and serve hot.

COOK'S TIP

You can store pesto in the refrigerator for about 4 weeks. Cover the surface of the pesto with olive oil before sealing the container or bottle, to prevent the basil from oxidizing and turning black.

Mediterranean Sauce

Delicious Mediterranean vegetables, cooked in rich tomato sauce, make an ideal topping for nutty whole-wheat pasta.

NUTRITIONAL INFORMATION

Calories ...... .492	Sugars 13g
Protein 15g	Fat 16g
Carbohydrate ...77g	Saturates 5g

🍤 🍤 🍤

🥔 10 mins   🕐 40 mins

SERVES 4

INGREDIENTS

2 tbsp olive oil

1 large red onion, chopped

2 garlic cloves, finely chopped

1 tbsp lemon juice

4 baby eggplants, cut into fourths

2½ cups strained tomatoes

2 tsp superfine sugar

2 tbsp tomato paste

14 oz/400 g canned artichoke hearts, drained and halved

1 cup pitted black olives

12 oz/350 g dried spaghetti

2 tbsp butter

salt and pepper

sprigs of fresh basil, to garnish

olive bread, to serve

and stir in the superfine sugar and tomato paste. Bring to a boil, then lower the heat and simmer, stirring occasionally, for 20 minutes.

3 Gently stir in the artichoke hearts and black olives and cook for 5 minutes.

4 Meanwhile, bring a large pan of lightly salted water to a boil. Add the spaghetti and the remaining oil and cook for 7–8 minutes, or until tender but still firm to the bite.

5 Drain the spaghetti and toss with the butter. Transfer the spaghetti to a large serving dish.

6 Pour the vegetable sauce over the spaghetti and garnish with the sprigs of fresh basil. Serve immediately with olive bread.

1 Heat half of the olive oil in a large skillet. Add the onion, garlic, lemon juice, and eggplants and cook over low heat for 4–5 minutes, or until the onion and eggplants are lightly golden brown.

2 Pour in the strained tomatoes, season to taste with salt and black pepper,

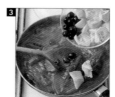

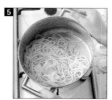

Garlic Walnut Sauce

A rich pasta sauce for garlic lovers everywhere, this is quick and easy to prepare and full of flavor.

NUTRITIONAL INFORMATION

Calories	474	Sugars	.........3g
Protein	........16g	Fat	..........24g
Carbohydrate	...52g	Saturates	.......9g

🥗 20 mins   🕐 15 mins

SERVES 4

INGREDIENTS

2 tbsp walnut oil

1 bunch of scallions, sliced

2 garlic cloves, thinly sliced

3¼ cups sliced mushrooms

1 lb/450 g fresh green tagliatelle

8 oz/225 g frozen spinach, thawed and drained

½ cup fullfat soft cheese with garlic and herbs

4 tbsp light cream

½ cup chopped, unsalted pistachios

2 tbsp shredded fresh basil

salt and pepper

sprigs of fresh basil, to garnish

Italian bread, such as focaccia or ciabatta, to serve

1 Heat the walnut oil in a large skillet. Add the scallions and garlic and cook for 1 minute, until just softened.

2 Add the mushrooms to the skillet, stir well, cover, and cook over low heat for about 5 minutes, until just softened but not browned.

3 Meanwhile, bring a large pan of lightly salted water to a boil. Add the tagliatelle, bring back to a boil, and cook for 3–5 minutes, or until tender but still firm to the bite. Drain the tagliatelle thoroughly and return to the pan.

4 Add the spinach to the skillet and heat through for 1–2 minutes. Add the cheese and heat until slightly melted. Stir in the cream and cook gently, without letting the mixture come to a boil, until warmed through.

5 Pour the sauce over the pasta, season to taste with salt and pepper, and mix well. Heat through gently, stirring constantly, for 2–3 minutes.

6 Transfer the pasta to a warmed serving dish and sprinkle with the pistachios and shredded basil. Garnish with the fresh basil sprigs and serve immediately with focaccia, ciabatta, or other Italian bread of your choice.

Hot Zucchini Sauce

This is a really fresh-tasting sauce, made with zucchini and cream.
This dish is ideal with a crisp white wine and some crusty bread.

NUTRITIONAL INFORMATION

Calories	502	Sugars	........5g
Protein	........16g	Fat	.........30g
Carbohydrate	...44g	Saturates	.......9g

 10 mins   20 mins

SERVES 4

I N G R E D I E N T S

1 lb 8 oz/675 g zucchini

6 tbsp olive oil

3 garlic cloves, crushed

3 tbsp chopped fresh basil

2 fresh red chiles, seeded and sliced

juice of 1 large lemon

5 tbsp light cream

4 tbsp grated Parmesan cheese

8 oz/225 g dried tagliatelle

salt and pepper

crusty bread, to serve

1 Using a swivel vegetable peeler, slice the zucchini into thin ribbons.

2 Heat the oil in a skillet and cook the garlic for 30 seconds.

COOK'S TIP

You can use lime juice instead of the lemon juice. Since limes are usually smaller, squeeze the juice from 2 fruits.

3 Add the zucchini ribbons and cook over low heat, stirring constantly, for 5–7 minutes.

4 Stir in the basil, chiles, lemon juice, cream, and Parmesan cheese, and season with salt and pepper to taste. Keep warm over very low heat while the pasta is cooking.

5 Bring a large pan of lightly salted water to a boil. Add the pasta, bring back to a boil, and cook for 8–10 minutes, until tender but still firm to the bite. Drain thoroughly and put the pasta in a warm serving bowl.

6 Pile the zucchini sauce on top of the pasta and serve with crusty bread.

Creamy Mushroom Sauce

This easy vegetarian sauce is ideal for busy people with little time to spare, but very good taste!

NUTRITIONAL INFORMATION

Calories	763	Sugars	........11g
Protein	........17g	Fat	..........38g
Carbohydrate	...93g	Saturates	......20g

10 mins   35 mins

SERVES 4

I N G R E D I E N T S

4 tbsp butter

2 tbsp olive oil

6 shallots, sliced

6 cups sliced white mushrooms

1 tsp all-purpose flour

⅔ cup heavy cream

2 tbsp port

4 oz/115 g sun-dried tomatoes, chopped

pinch of freshly grated nutmeg

1 lb/450 g dried spaghetti

1 tbsp chopped fresh parsley

salt and pepper

6 triangles of fried white bread, to serve

1 Heat the butter and half of the olive oil in a large pan. Add the sliced shallots and cook over medium heat for 3 minutes. Add the mushrooms and cook over low heat for 2 minutes. Season to taste with salt and black pepper, then sprinkle over the flour and cook, stirring constantly, for 1 minute.

2 Gradually stir in the cream and port, then add the sun-dried tomatoes and a pinch of grated nutmeg. Cook over low heat for 8 minutes.

3 Meanwhile, bring a large pan of lightly salted water to a boil. Add the spaghetti and remaining olive oil and cook for 12–14 minutes, or until tender but still firm to the bite.

4 Drain the spaghetti and return to the pan. Pour over the mushroom sauce and cook for 3 minutes. Transfer the spaghetti and mushroom sauce to a large serving plate and sprinkle over the chopped parsley. Serve with crispy triangles of fried bread.

VARIATION

If you like the sound of this recipe but do not have any port available, you can use 2 tablespoons of dry white wine instead.

Walnut & Olive Sauce

This vegetarian sauce is mouthwateringly light and excellent with pasta. The quantities given here will make a lunch for four or an appetizer for six.

NUTRITIONAL INFORMATION

Calories 833	Sugars 5g
Protein 20g	Fat 66g
Carbohydrate . . .44g	Saturates 15g

🍳 15 mins   🕙 10 mins

SERVES 4–6

INGREDIENTS

2 thick slices whole-wheat bread, crusts removed

1¼ cups milk

2½ cups shelled walnuts

2 garlic cloves, minced

1 cup pitted black olives

⅔ cup freshly grated Parmesan cheese

½ cup extra-virgin olive oil

⅔ cup heavy cream

1 lb/450 g fresh fettuccine

salt and pepper

2–3 tbsp chopped fresh parsley

1 Put the bread in a shallow dish. Pour over the milk and let soak until the liquid has been absorbed.

2 Spread the walnuts out on a cookie sheet and toast in a preheated oven

at 375°F/190°C for about 5 minutes, or until golden. Let cool.

3 Put the soaked bread, walnuts, garlic, olives, Parmesan, and 6 tablespoons of the olive oil in a food processor and work to make a paste. Season to taste with salt and black pepper and stir in the cream.

4 Bring a large pan of lightly salted water to a boil. Add the fettuccine

and 1 tablespoon of the remaining oil and cook for 2–3 minutes, or until tender but still firm to the bite. Drain the fettuccine thoroughly and toss with the remaining olive oil.

5 Divide the cooked fettuccine between individual serving plates and spoon the walnut and olive sauce on top. Sprinkle over the fresh parsley and serve.

COOK'S TIP

Parmesan quickly loses its pungency and bite. It is better to buy small quantities and grate it yourself. Wrapped in foil, it will keep in the refrigerator for several months.

Buttered Pea & Cheese Sauce

This delicious sauce is served with *paglia e fieno* ("straw and hay" pasta), which refers to the colors of the pasta when mixed together.

NUTRITIONAL INFORMATION

Calories 699	Sugars 7g	
Protein 26g	Fat 39g	
Carbohydrate . . .65g	Saturates 23g	

 10 mins   10 mins

SERVES 4

I N G R E D I E N T S

4 tbsp butter

1 lb/450 g fresh peas, shelled

scant 1 cup heavy cream

1 lb/450 g mixed fresh green and white spaghetti or tagliatelle

⅔ cup freshly grated Parmesan cheese, plus extra to serve

pinch of freshly grated nutmeg

salt and pepper

1 Melt the butter in a large pan. Add the peas and cook over low heat for 2–3 minutes.

2 Pour ⅔ cup of the cream into the pan, bring to a boil, and then simmer for 1–1½ minutes, or until slightly thickened. Remove the pan from the heat.

3 Meanwhile, bring a large pan of lightly salted water to a boil. Add the spaghetti or tagliatelle, bring back to a boil, and cook for 2–3 minutes, or until just tender but still firm to the bite. Remove the pan from the heat, drain the pasta thoroughly, and return to the pan.

4 Add the peas and cream sauce to the pasta. Return the pan to the heat and add the remaining cream and the Parmesan cheese and season to taste with nutmeg and salt and pepper.

5 While heating through, use 2 forks to toss the pasta gently so that it is coated with the peas and cream sauce.

6 Transfer the pasta to a warmed serving dish and serve immediately, with extra Parmesan cheese.

VARIATION

Cook 5 oz/140 g sliced button or oyster mushrooms in 4 tablespoons butter over low heat for 4–5 minutes. Stir into the peas and cream sauce just before adding to the pasta in step 4.

Chile & Bell Pepper Sauce

This roasted bell pepper and chile sauce is sweet and spicy—the perfect combination for those who like to add just a little spice to life!

NUTRITIONAL INFORMATION

Calories	423	Sugars	.........5g
Protein	.........9g	Fat	..........27g
Carbohydrate	...38g	Saturates	.......4g

 25 mins 🕐 30 mins

SERVES 4

I N G R E D I E N T S

2 red bell peppers, halved and seeded

1 small, fresh, red chile

4 tomatoes, halved

2 garlic cloves

½ cup ground almonds

generous ⅓ cup olive oil

1 lb 8 oz/675 g fresh pasta or 12 oz/350 g dried pasta

fresh oregano leaves, to garnish

  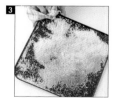

1 Place the bell peppers, skin side up, on a cookie sheet with the chile and tomatoes. Cook under a preheated broiler for 15 minutes, or until charred. After 10 minutes, turn the tomatoes over, skin side up. Place the bell peppers and chiles in a plastic bag and set aside for 10 minutes.

2 Peel the skins from the bell peppers and chile and slice the flesh into strips. Peel the garlic, and peel and seed the tomato halves.

3 Place the ground almonds on a cookie sheet and place under the broiler for 2–3 minutes, until golden.

4 In a food processor, process the bell peppers, chile, garlic, and tomatoes to make a puree. With the motor still running, slowly add the olive oil through the feeder tube to form a thick sauce. Alternatively, mash the mixture with a fork and beat in the olive oil, drop by drop.

5 Stir the toasted ground almonds into the mixture. Warm the sauce in a pan, until it is heated through.

6 Bring a large pan of lightly salted water to a boil. Add the pasta, bring back to a boil, and cook for 3–5 minutes if using fresh pasta, or 8–10 minutes if using dried pasta. Drain the pasta thoroughly and transfer to a serving dish. Pour over the sauce and toss to mix. Garnish with the fresh oregano leaves and serve.

VARIATION

Add 2 tablespoons of red wine vinegar to the sauce and use as a dressing for a cold pasta salad, if you wish.

Fragrant Eggplant Sauce

Prepare the marinated eggplants well in advance so that, when you are ready to eat, all you have to do is cook the pasta.

NUTRITIONAL INFORMATION

Calories 378	Sugars 3g	
Protein 12g	Fat 30g	
Carbohydrate ...16g	Saturates 3g	

12¼ hrs   15 mins

SERVES 4

I N G R E D I E N T S

⅔ cup vegetable bouillon

⅔ cup white wine vinegar

2 tsp balsamic vinegar

3 tbsp olive oil

sprig of fresh oregano

1 lb/450 g eggplants, peeled and thinly sliced

14 oz/400 g dried linguine

M A R I N A D E

2 tbsp extra-virgin olive oil

2 garlic cloves, crushed

2 tbsp chopped fresh oregano

2 tbsp finely chopped roasted almonds

2 tbsp diced red bell pepper

2 tbsp lime juice

grated rind and juice of 1 orange

salt and pepper

1 Put the vegetable bouillon, wine vinegar, and balsamic vinegar into a pan and bring to a boil over low heat. Add 2 teaspoons of the olive oil and the sprig of fresh oregano and simmer gently for about 1 minute.

2 Add the eggplant slices to the pan, remove from the heat, and set aside for 10 minutes.

3 Meanwhile, make the marinade. Combine the oil, garlic, fresh oregano, almonds, red bell pepper, lime juice, and orange rind and juice in a large bowl and season to taste with salt and pepper.

4 Using a slotted spoon, carefully remove the eggplant slices from the pan and drain well. Add the eggplant slices to the marinade, mixing well to coat. Cover with plastic wrap and set aside in the refrigerator for about 12 hours.

5 Bring a large pan of lightly salted water to a boil. Add half of the remaining oil and the linguine. Bring back to a boil and cook for 8–10 minutes, until just tender but still firm to the bite.

6 Drain the pasta thoroughly and toss with the remaining oil while it is still warm. Arrange the pasta on a serving plate with the eggplant slices and the marinade and serve immediately.

Tuna & Anchovy Sauce

The delicious parsley sauce in this recipe enhances the classic Italian combination of pasta and tuna.

NUTRITIONAL INFORMATION

Calories	1065	Sugars	3g
Protein	27g	Fat	85g
Carbohydrate	52g	Saturates	18g

10 mins   15 mins

SERVES 4

INGREDIENTS

7 oz/200 g canned tuna, drained

2¼ oz/60 g canned anchovies, drained

1 cup olive oil

1 cup coarsely chopped flatleaf parsley

⅔ cup crème fraîche or unsweetened yogurt

1 lb/450 g dried spaghetti

2 tbsp butter

salt and pepper

black olives, to garnish

warm crusty bread, to serve

1 Remove any bones from the tuna. Put the tuna into a food processor or blender. Add the anchovies, all but 1 tablespoon of the olive oil, and all the flatleaf parsley. Process until the sauce is very smooth.

2 Spoon the crème fraîche or yogurt into the food processor or blender and process again for a few seconds to blend thoroughly. Season with salt and pepper to taste.

3 Bring a large pan of lightly salted water to a boil. Add the spaghetti and the remaining olive oil and cook for 8–10 minutes, or until tender but still firm to the bite.

4 Drain the spaghetti, return to the pan, and place over medium heat. Add the butter and toss well to coat. Spoon in the sauce and quickly toss into the spaghetti, mixing well using 2 forks.

5 Remove the pan from the heat and divide the spaghetti between warm individual serving plates. Garnish with olives and serve with warm, crusty bread.

VARIATION

If desired, you could add 1-2 garlic cloves to the sauce, substitute ½ cup chopped fresh basil for half the parsley, and garnish with capers instead of black olives.

Smoked Salmon Cream Sauce

This luxurious sauce is made in moments, and can be used to astonish and delight any unexpected guests.

NUTRITIONAL INFORMATION

Calories	949	Sugars	6g
Protein	26g	Fat	49g
Carbohydrate	86g	Saturates	27g

5–10 mins   5 mins

SERVES 4

I N G R E D I E N T S

1 lb/450 g dried buckwheat spaghetti

2 tbsp olive oil

1¼ cups heavy cream

⅔ cup whiskey or brandy

4½ oz/125 g smoked salmon

pinch of cayenne pepper

black pepper

2 tbsp chopped fresh cilantro or parsley

½ cup feta cheese, well drained and crumbled

fresh cilantro or parsley leaves, to garnish

1 Bring a large pan of lightly salted water to a boil. Add the spaghetti and half of the olive oil and cook until tender but still firm to the bite. Drain the spaghetti, return to the pan, and sprinkle over the remaining olive oil. Cover, shake the pan, set aside, and keep warm.

2 Pour the cream into a small pan and bring to simmering point, but do not let it boil. Pour the whiskey or brandy into another small pan and bring to simmering point, but do not let it boil. Remove both pans from the heat and mix the cream with the whiskey or brandy.

3 Cut the smoked salmon into thin strips and add to the cream sauce. Season to taste with cayenne and black pepper. Just before serving, stir in the chopped fresh cilantro or parsley.

4 Transfer the spaghetti to a warm serving dish, pour over the sauce, and toss thoroughly with 2 large forks. Scatter over the crumbled feta cheese, garnish with the cilantro or parsley leaves, and serve immediately.

COOK'S TIP

Serve this rich and luxurious dish with salad greens tossed in a lemon-flavored dressing.

Sardine & Fennel Sauce

This is a very quick sauce and is ideal paired with pasta for midweek suppers because it is so simple to prepare, yet packed full of flavor.

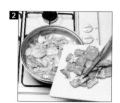

NUTRITIONAL INFORMATION

Calories . . . . . . .547 Sugars 5g
Protein . . . . .23g Fat 23g
Carbohydrate . . .68g Saturates 3g

10 mins   12 mins

SERVES 4

I N G R E D I E N T S

| 8 sardines, filleted |
| 1 fennel bulb |
| 4 tbsp olive oil |
| 3 garlic cloves, sliced |
| 1 tsp chili flakes |
| 12 oz/350 g dried linguine |
| ½ tsp finely grated lemon rind |
| 1 tbsp lemon juice |
| 2 tbsp pine nuts, toasted |
| 2 tbsp chopped fresh parsley |
| salt and pepper |

1 Wash the sardine fillets and pat dry on paper towels. Coarsely chop them into large pieces and set aside. Trim the fennel bulb and slice very thinly.

COOK'S TIP

Reserve a couple of tablespoons of the pasta cooking water and add to the pasta with the sauce if the mixture seems a little dry.

2 Heat 2 tablespoons of the olive oil in a large, heavy skillet and add the garlic and chili flakes. Cook for 1 minute, then add the fennel slices. Cook over medium-high heat, stirring occasionally, for 4–5 minutes, until softened. Lower the heat, add the sardine pieces, and cook for another 3–4 minutes, until just cooked.

3 Meanwhile, bring a pan of lightly salted water to a boil. Add the pasta,

bring back to a boil, and cook for about 8–10 minutes, until tender but still firm to the bite. Drain well and return to the pan.

4 Add the lemon rind, lemon juice, pine nuts, and parsley to the sardine sauce and toss together. Season to taste with salt and pepper. Add to the pasta with the remaining olive oil and toss together gently. Transfer to a warmed serving dish and serve immediately.

Sicilian Sauce

This Sicilian sauce of anchovies mixed with pine nuts, golden raisins, and tomatoes is delicious with all types of pasta.

NUTRITIONAL INFORMATION

Calories 286	Sugars 14g
Protein 11g	Fat 8g
Carbohydrate . . .46g	Saturates 1g

🍲 25 mins 🕐 30 mins

SERVES 4

I N G R E D I E N T S

1 lb/450 g tomatoes, halved

1 oz/25 g pine nuts

1¾ oz/50 g golden raisins

1¾ oz/50 g canned anchovies, drained and halved lengthwise

2 tbsp concentrated tomato paste

1lb 8 oz/675 g fresh penne or 12 oz/350 g dried penne

1 Cook the tomatoes under a preheated broiler for about 10 minutes. Let cool. Once cool enough to handle, peel off the skin and dice the flesh.

2 Place the pine nuts on a cookie sheet and lightly toast under the broiler for 2–3 minutes, or until golden.

3 Soak the golden raisins in a bowl of warm water for about 20 minutes. Drain the golden raisins thoroughly.

4 Place the tomatoes, toasted pine nuts, and golden raisins in a small pan and heat gently.

5 Add the anchovies and tomato paste, heating the sauce for an additional 2–3 minutes, or until hot.

6 Cook the pasta in a pan of lightly salted boiling water according to the instructions on the package, or until tender but still firm to the bite. Drain thoroughly.

7 Transfer the pasta to a serving plate and serve with the hot sauce.

COOK'S TIP

If you are making fresh pasta, remember that pasta dough prefers warm conditions and responds well to handling. Do not let chill and do not use a marble counter for kneading.

Spinach & Anchovy Sauce

This colorful light sauce can be paired with different types of pasta, including fettuccine, spaghetti, and linguine.

NUTRITIONAL INFORMATION		
Calories 619	Sugars 5g	
Protein 21g	Fat 31g	
Carbohydrate ...67g	Saturates 3g	

 10 mins 25 mins

SERVES 4

I N G R E D I E N T S

2 lb/900 g fresh, young spinach leaves

14 oz/400 g dried fettuccine

5 tbsp olive oil

3 tbsp pine nuts

3 garlic cloves, crushed

8 canned anchovy fillets, drained
  and chopped

salt

1 Trim off any tough spinach stalks. Rinse the spinach leaves and place them in a large pan with only the water that is clinging to them after washing. Cover and cook over high heat, shaking the pan from time, until the spinach has wilted but retains its color. Drain well, set aside, and keep warm.

COOK'S TIP

If you are in a hurry, you can use frozen spinach. Thaw and drain it thoroughly, pressing out as much moisture as possible. Cut the leaves into strips and add to the dish with the anchovies in step 4.

2 Bring a large pan of lightly salted water to a boil. Add the fettuccine, bring back to a boil, and cook for 8–10 minutes, until it is just tender but still firm to the bite.

3 Meanwhile, heat 4 tablespoons of the olive oil in a pan. Add the pine nuts and cook until golden. Remove the pine nuts from the pan with a slotted spoon and set aside until required.

4 Add the garlic to the pan and cook until golden. Add the anchovies and stir in the spinach. Cook, stirring constantly, for 2–3 minutes, until heated through. Return the pine nuts to the pan.

5 Drain the fettuccine, toss in the remaining olive oil, and transfer to a warm serving dish. Spoon the anchovy and spinach sauce over the fettuccine, toss lightly, and serve immediately.

Shrimp & Vegetable Sauce

Shelled shrimp from the freezer can become the star ingredient in this colorful and tasty sauce.

NUTRITIONAL INFORMATION

Calories 498	Sugars 5g
Protein 32g	Fat 23g
Carbohydrate . . .43g	Saturates 11g

🍲 30 mins   🕐 35 mins

SERVES 4

INGREDIENTS

8 oz/225 g dried spaghetti, broken into 6-inch/15-cm pieces

2 tbsp olive oil

1¼ cups chicken bouillon

1 tsp lemon juice

1 small cauliflower, cut into florets

2 carrots, thinly sliced

4 oz/115 g snow peas

4 tbsp butter

1 onion, sliced

8 oz/225 g zucchini, sliced

1 garlic clove, chopped

12 oz/350 g cooked, peeled shrimp

2 tbsp chopped fresh parsley

⅓ cup freshly grated Parmesan cheese

½ tsp paprika

salt and pepper

4 whole cooked shrimp, to garnish

1 Bring a pan of lightly salted water to a boil. Add the spaghetti and half of the olive oil and cook until tender, but still firm to the bite. Drain the spaghetti, then return to the pan and toss with the remaining olive oil. Cover and keep warm.

2 Bring the chicken bouillon and lemon juice to a boil. Add the cauliflower and carrots and cook for 3–4 minutes. Lift out of the pan and set aside. Add the snow peas to the pan and cook for 1–2 minutes. Remove and set aside with the other vegetables.

3 Melt half the butter in a skillet over medium heat. Add the onion and zucchini and cook for about 3 minutes. Add the garlic and peeled shrimp and cook for an additional 2–3 minutes, or until thoroughly heated through.

4 Add the reserved vegetables and heat through, stirring. Season to taste and stir in the remaining butter.

5 Transfer the spaghetti to a warm serving dish. Pour over the sauce and add the chopped parsley. Toss well with 2 forks until coated. Sprinkle over the Parmesan cheese and paprika, then garnish with the whole shrimp and serve immediately.

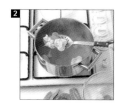

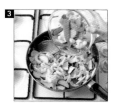

Saffron Mussel Sauce

Saffron is the most expensive spice in the world, but you only ever need a small quantity. This sauce is delicious with tagliatelle or other ribbon pasta.

NUTRITIONAL INFORMATION

Calories 854	Sugars 3g
Protein 43g	Fat 49g
Carbohydrate ...57g	Saturates 28g

15 mins   35 mins

SERVES 4

INGREDIENTS

2 lb 4 oz/1 kg mussels

²⁄₃ cup white wine

1 medium onion, finely chopped

2 tbsp butter

2 garlic cloves, ground

2 tsp cornstarch

1¼ cups heavy cream

pinch of saffron threads or saffron powder

1 egg yolk

juice of ½ lemon

1 lb/450 g dried tagliatelle

1 tbsp olive oil

salt and pepper

3 tbsp chopped fresh parsley, to garnish

1 Scrub and debeard the mussels under cold running water. Discard any that do not close when sharply tapped. Put the mussels in a pan with the wine and onion. Cover and cook over high heat, shaking the pan, for 5–8 minutes, or until the shells open.

2 Drain and reserve the cooking liquid. Discard any mussels that are still closed. Reserve a few mussels for the garnish and remove the remainder from their shells.

3 Strain the cooking liquid into a pan. Bring to a boil and reduce by about half. Remove the pan from the heat.

4 Melt the butter in a pan. Add the garlic and cook, stirring frequently, for 2 minutes, or until golden brown. Stir in the cornstarch and cook, stirring, for 1 minute. Gradually stir in the cooking liquid and the cream. Crush the saffron threads and add to the pan. Season with salt and pepper to taste and simmer over low heat for 2–3 minutes, or until thickened.

5 Stir in the egg yolk, lemon juice, and shelled mussels. Do not let the mixture boil.

6 Meanwhile, bring a pan of salted water to a boil. Add the pasta and oil and cook until tender, but still firm to the bite. Drain and transfer to a serving dish. Add the mussel sauce and toss. Garnish with the chopped parsley and reserved mussels and serve.

Seafood Sauce

Fresh clams are available from most good fish stores. If you prefer, use canned clams, which are less messy to eat but not so pretty to serve.

NUTRITIONAL INFORMATION

Calories	410	Sugars	1g
Protein	39g	Fat	9g
Carbohydrate	39g	Saturates	1g

 20 mins   🕐 20 mins

SERVES 4

INGREDIENTS

1 lb 8 oz/675 g fresh clams, or 10 oz/280 g canned clams, drained

2 tbsp olive oil

2 garlic cloves, finely chopped

14 oz/400 g mixed seafood, such as shrimp, squid, and mussels, defrosted if frozen

⅔ cup white wine

⅔ cup fish bouillon

1 lb 8 oz/675 g fresh pasta, or 12 oz/350 g dried pasta

2 tbsp chopped fresh tarragon

salt and pepper

1 If you are using fresh clams, scrub them clean and discard any that are already open.

2 Heat the oil in a large skillet. Add the garlic and the clams to the pan and cook for 2 minutes, shaking the pan to ensure that all of the clams are coated in the oil.

3 Add the remaining seafood to the pan and cook for an additional 2 minutes.

4 Pour the wine and bouillon over the mixed seafood and garlic and bring to a boil. Cover the pan, then lower the heat and let simmer for 8–10 minutes, or until the shells open. Discard any clams or mussels that do not open.

5 Meanwhile, cook the pasta in a pan of boiling water according to the instructions on the package, or until tender but still firm to the bite. Drain.

6 Stir the tarragon into the sauce and season to taste.

7 Transfer the pasta to a serving plate and pour over the sauce.

VARIATION
Red clam sauce can be made by adding ½ cup tomato paste to the sauce along with the bouillon in step 4. Follow the same cooking method.

Clam Sauce

This is a cook-in-a-hurry recipe that transforms pantry ingredients into a sauce with style.

NUTRITIONAL INFORMATION

Calories	392	Sugars	.........2g
Protein	........23g	Fat	..........15g
Carbohydrate	...37g	Saturates	......6g

 5 mins   20 mins

SERVES 4

I N G R E D I E N T S

14 oz/400 g vermicelli, spaghetti, or other long pasta

2 tbsp butter

salt

sprigs of fresh basil, to garnish

2 tbsp flaked Parmesan, to serve

S A U C E

1 tbsp olive oil

2 onions, chopped

2 garlic cloves, chopped

two 7-oz/200-g jars clams in brine

½ cup white wine

4 tbsp chopped fresh parsley

½ tsp dried oregano

pinch of grated nutmeg

pepper

1 Bring a large pan of lightly salted water to a boil. Add the pasta, bring back to a boil, and cook for 8–10 minutes, until tender but still firm to the bite. Drain well, return to the pan, and add the butter. Cover and shake. Set the pan aside and keep warm.

2 To make the clam sauce, heat the oil in a pan. Add the onions and cook over low heat, stirring occasionally, for 5 minutes, until softened. Stir in the garlic and cook for another minute.

3 Strain the liquid from 1 jar of clams and pour it into the pan. Strain the liquid from the other jar of clams and discard. Reserve the clams.

4 Add the wine to the pan. Bring to simmering point, stirring constantly, and simmer for 3 minutes.

5 Add the clams and herbs to the pan and season to taste with nutmeg and pepper. Lower the heat and cook until the sauce is heated through.

6 Transfer the pasta to a warmed serving platter and pour the clam sauce over it. Season with salt to taste.

7 Garnish with the basil and sprinkle over the Parmesan. Serve hot.

Spicy Crab Sauce

This sauce is probably one of the simplest in the book, yet the flavor is as impressive as a sauce over which you have slaved for hours.

NUTRITIONAL INFORMATION

Calories 488   Sugars 3g
Protein . . . . .13g   Fat 19g
Carbohydrate . . .65g   Saturates 3g

15 mins   8–10 mins

SERVES 4

I N G R E D I E N T S

1 dressed crab, about 1 lb/450 g including
   the shell

12 oz/350 g dried spaghettini

6 tbsp extra-virgin olive oil

1 fresh red chile, seeded and
   finely chopped

2 garlic cloves, finely chopped

3 tbsp chopped fresh parsley

2 tbsp lemon juice

1 tsp finely grated lemon rind

salt and pepper

lemon wedges, to garnish

1 Scoop the meat from the crab shell into a bowl. Mix the white and brown meat lightly together and set aside.

2 Bring a large pan of lightly salted water to a boil. Add the pasta, bring back to a boil, and cook for 8–10 minutes, until tender but still firm to the bite. Drain well and return to the pan.

3 Meanwhile, heat 2 tablespoons of the olive oil in a skillet. Add the chile and garlic. Cook for 30 seconds, then add the crab meat, parsley, lemon juice, and lemon rind. Stir-fry over low heat for another minute, until the crab meat is just heated through.

4 Add the crab sauce to the pasta with the remaining olive oil and season to taste with salt and pepper. Toss together thoroughly, transfer to a warmed serving dish, and serve immediately, garnished with lemon wedges.

COOK'S TIP

If you prefer to buy your own fresh crab you will need a large crab weighing about 2 lb 4 oz/1 kg.

Bolognese Sauce

You can also use this classic meat sauce for baked pasta dishes such as lasagna and cannelloni.

NUTRITIONAL INFORMATION

Calories 732	Sugars 15g
Protein 39g	Fat 20g
Carbohydrate . . . 96g	Saturates 5g

5 mins 1¼ hrs

SERVES 4

I N G R E D I E N T S

3 tbsp olive oil

2 garlic cloves, crushed

1 large onion, finely chopped

1 carrot, diced

2 cups lean ground beef, veal, or chicken

3 oz/85 g chicken livers, finely chopped

3½ oz/100 g lean prosciutto, diced

⅔ cup Marsala

10 oz/280 g canned chopped
   plum tomatoes

1 tbsp chopped fresh basil leaves

2 tbsp tomato paste

salt and pepper

1 lb/450 g dried spaghetti

1 Heat 2 tablespoons of the olive oil in a large pan. Add the garlic, onion, and carrot and cook for 6 minutes.

VARIATION

Chicken livers are an essential ingredient in a classic Bolognese sauce, to which they add richness. However, if you prefer not to use them, you can substitute the same quantity of ground beef.

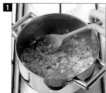  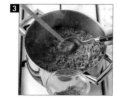

2 Add the ground beef, veal, or chicken to the pan, and the chicken livers and prosciutto. Cook over medium heat for 12 minutes, until well browned.

3 Stir in the Marsala, tomatoes, basil, and tomato paste and cook, stirring, for 4 minutes. Season to taste with salt and pepper. Cover the pan and simmer for about 30 minutes.

4 Remove the lid from the pan, stir, and simmer for another 15 minutes.

5 Meanwhile, bring a large pan of lightly salted water to a boil. Add the spaghetti and the remaining oil and cook for about 12 minutes, or until tender but still firm to the bite. Drain and transfer to a serving dish. Pour the sauce over the pasta and serve hot.

Tarragon Meatball Sauce

This well-loved Italian sauce is famous across the world. Make the most of it by using high-quality steak for the meatballs.

NUTRITIONAL INFORMATION

Calories .... 665 Sugars 9g
Protein .... 39g Fat 24g
Carbohydrate ... 77g Saturates 8g

 45 mins   🕐 1¼ hrs

SERVES 4

INGREDIENTS

2½ cups brown bread crumbs

⅔ cup milk

2 tbsp butter

3 tbsp whole-wheat flour

scant 1 cup beef bouillon

14 oz/400 g canned chopped tomatoes

2 tbsp tomato paste

1 tsp sugar

1 tbsp finely chopped fresh tarragon

1 large onion, chopped

4 cups ground steak

1 tsp paprika

4 tbsp olive oil

1 lb/450 g fresh spaghetti

salt and pepper

sprigs of fresh tarragon, to garnish

1 Place the brown bread crumbs in a bowl, add the milk and set aside to soak for about 30 minutes.

2 Melt half of the butter in a pan. Add the flour and cook, stirring constantly, for 2 minutes. Gradually stir in the beef bouillon and cook, stirring constantly, for another 5 minutes. Add the tomatoes, tomato paste, sugar, and tarragon. Season well and simmer for 25 minutes.

3 Mix the onion, ground steak, and paprika into the bread crumbs, and season with salt and pepper to taste. Shape the mixture into 14 meatballs.

4 Heat the oil and remaining butter in a skillet and cook the meatballs, turning, until brown all over. Place in a deep casserole, pour over the tomato sauce, cover, and bake in a preheated oven, 350°F/180°C, for 25 minutes.

5 Bring a large pan of lightly salted water to a boil. Add the fresh spaghetti, bring back to a boil, and cook for about 2–3 minutes, or until tender but firm to the bite.

6 Meanwhile, remove the meatballs from the oven and let cool for 3 minutes. Serve the meatballs and their sauce with the spaghetti, garnished with sprigs of fresh tarragon.

Carbonara Sauce

Ensure that all of the cooked ingredients are as hot as possible before adding the eggs, so that they cook on contact.

NUTRITIONAL INFORMATION	
Calories 1092	Sugars 9g
Protein 37g	Fat 69g
Carbohydrate ... 86g	Saturates 36g

🍳 10 mins · ⏱ 15 mins

SERVES 4

INGREDIENTS

15 oz/425 g dried spaghetti

1 tbsp olive oil

1 large onion, thinly sliced

2 garlic cloves, chopped

6 oz/175 g rindless bacon, cut into thin strips

2 tbsp butter

2½ cups sliced mushrooms

1¼ cups heavy cream

3 eggs, beaten

generous 1 cup freshly grated Parmesan

salt and pepper

sprigs of fresh sage, to garnish

freshly grated Parmesan, to serve (optional)

1 Warm a large serving dish or bowl. Bring a large pan of lightly salted water to a boil. Add the spaghetti, bring back to a boil, and cook for 8–10 minutes, until tender but still firm to the bite. Drain well, return to the pan, and keep warm.

2 Meanwhile, heat the olive oil in a skillet over medium heat. Add the onion and cook, stirring occasionally, for 2–3 minutes, until translucent. Add the garlic and bacon and cook until the bacon is crisp. Transfer to the warm dish or bowl.

3 Melt the butter in the skillet. Add the mushrooms and cook over medium heat, stirring occasionally, for 3–4 minutes, until tender. Return the bacon mixture to the skillet. Cover and keep warm.

4 Combine the cream, eggs, and cheese in a large bowl, and season to taste with salt and pepper.

5 Working very quickly, tip the spaghetti into the bacon and mushroom mixture and pour over the eggs. Toss the spaghetti quickly into the egg and cream mixture, using 2 forks, and serve immediately. If you wish, serve with extra grated Parmesan cheese.

COOK'S TIP

The key to success with this recipe is not to overcook the egg. That is why it is important to keep all the ingredients hot enough just to cook the egg and to work rapidly to avoid scrambling it.

Sun-Dried Tomato Sauce

There is an appetizing contrast of textures and flavors in this satisfying sauce, which is an excellent accompaniment for the meatballs and pasta.

NUTRITIONAL INFORMATION

Calories 910   Sugars 13g
Protein . . . . .40g   Fat 54g
Carbohydrate . . .65g   Saturates 19g

 🗑 🗑 🗑

🍲 45 mins   🕐 1 hr 5 mins

SERVES 4

I N G R E D I E N T S

1 lb 2 oz/500 g ground lean beef

1 cup soft white bread crumbs

1 garlic clove, crushed

2 tbsp chopped fresh parsley

1 tsp dried oregano

pinch of freshly grated nutmeg

¼ tsp ground coriander

⅔ cup freshly grated Parmesan cheese

2–3 tbsp milk

all-purpose flour, for dusting

3 tbsp olive oil

14 oz/400 g dried tagliatelle

2 tbsp butter, diced

salt and pepper

S A U C E

3 tbsp olive oil

2 large onions, sliced

2 celery stalks, thinly sliced

2 garlic cloves, chopped

14 oz/400 g canned chopped tomatoes

4½ oz/125 g sun-dried tomatoes in oil, drained and chopped

2 tbsp tomato paste

1 tbsp molasses sugar

about ⅔ cup white wine or water

1 To make the sauce, heat the oil in a skillet. Add the onions and celery and cook until translucent. Add the garlic and cook for 1 minute. Stir in all the tomatoes, tomato paste, sugar, and wine or water, and season to taste with salt and pepper. Bring to a boil and simmer for 10 minutes.

2 Meanwhile, break up the meat in a bowl with a wooden spoon, until it becomes a sticky paste. Stir in the bread crumbs, garlic, herbs, and spices. Stir in the cheese and enough milk to make a firm paste. Flour your hands, take large spoonfuls of the mixture, and shape it into 12 balls. Heat the oil in a skillet and cook the meatballs for 5–6 minutes, until browned.

3 Pour the tomato sauce over the meatballs. Lower the heat, cover the pan, and simmer for 30 minutes, turning once or twice. Add a little extra wine or water if the sauce is beginning to become dry.

4 Bring a large pan of lightly salted water to a boil. Add the pasta, bring back to a boil, and cook for 8–10 minutes, until tender but still firm to the bite. Drain the pasta, then turn into a warmed serving dish, dot with the butter, and toss with 2 forks. Spoon the meatballs and sauce over the pasta and serve immediately.

Bacon & Tomato Sauce

As this sauce cooks, the mouthwatering aroma of bacon, sweet tomatoes, and oregano is a feast in itself.

NUTRITIONAL INFORMATION

Calories 431	Sugars 8g
Protein 10g	Fat 9g
Carbohydrate . . . 34g	Saturates 14g

🥔 10 mins   🕐 35 mins

SERVES 4

INGREDIENTS

2 lb/900 g small, sweet tomatoes

6 slices rindless smoked bacon

4 tbsp butter

1 onion, chopped

1 garlic clove, crushed

4 sprigs of fresh oregano, finely chopped

1 lb/450 g dried orecchiette

1 tbsp olive oil

salt and pepper

freshly grated romano cheese, to serve

1 Blanch the tomatoes in boiling water. Drain, skin, and seed the tomatoes, then coarsely chop the flesh.

2 Using a sharp knife, chop the bacon into even-size small dice.

3 Melt the butter in a pan. Add the bacon and cook until it is golden.

4 Add the onion and garlic and cook over medium heat for 5–7 minutes, until just softened.

5 Add the tomatoes and oregano to the pan and then season to taste with salt and pepper. Lower the heat and simmer gently for 10–12 minutes.

6 Bring a large pan of lightly salted water to a boil. Add the orecchiette and oil and cook for 12 minutes, or until just tender but still firm to the bite. Drain and transfer to a warm serving bowl.

7 Spoon the bacon and tomato sauce over the pasta, toss to coat, and serve with the romano cheese.

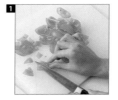

COOK'S TIP

For an authentic Italian flavor, use pancetta instead of ordinary bacon. Pancetta is streaked with fat and adds rich undertones of flavor to many traditional dishes. It is available smoked or unsmoked from large stores and delicatessens.

Pumpkin Sauce

This unusual pasta sauce comes from the Emilia Romagna region of Italy. Why not serve it with Lambrusco, the local wine?

NUTRITIONAL INFORMATION

Calories	559	Sugars	7g
Protein	17g	Fat	32g
Carbohydrate	55g	Saturates	14g

5 mins   20–25 mins

SERVES 4

I N G R E D I E N T S

1 lb 2 oz/500 g pumpkin or butternut squash, peeled and seeded

3 tbsp olive oil

1 onion, finely chopped

2 garlic cloves, crushed

4–6 tbsp chopped fresh parsley

pinch of freshly grated nutmeg

about 1¼ cups chicken bouillon or vegetable bouillon

4 oz/115 g prosciutto, cut into small pieces

9 oz/250 g dried tagliatelle

⅔ cup heavy cream

salt and pepper

freshly grated Parmesan, to serve

3 Add the pumpkin or squash pieces and cook for 2–3 minutes. Season to taste with nutmeg, and salt and pepper.

4 Add half the bouillon to the pan, bring to a boil, cover, and simmer for about 10 minutes, or until the pumpkin or squash is tender. Add more bouillon whenever the pumpkin or squash is becoming dry and looks as if it might be about to burn.

5 Add the prosciutto to the pan and cook, stirring, for another 2 minutes.

6 Meanwhile, bring a large pan of lightly salted water to a boil. Add the tagliatelle and the remaining oil and cook for 12 minutes, or until tender but still firm to the bite. Drain the pasta and transfer to a warm serving dish.

7 Stir the cream into the pumpkin and ham sauce and heat well through. Spoon the mixture over the tagliatelle, sprinkle over the remaining parsley to garnish, and serve while still hot. Serve the grated Parmesan separately.

1 Cut the pumpkin or butternut squash in half and scoop out the seeds with a spoon. Cut the pumpkin or squash into ½-inch/1-cm dice.

2 Heat 2 tablespoons of the olive oil in a large pan. Add the onion and garlic and cook over low heat for 3 minutes, until soft. Add half the parsley and cook for 1 minute.

Creamy Chicken Sauce

This creamy chicken sauce served with spinach ribbon noodles makes a very appetizing and satisfying dish.

NUTRITIONAL INFORMATION

Calories 853	Sugars 6g
Protein 32g	Fat 71g
Carbohydrate . . .23g	Saturates 34g

 30 mins   25 mins

SERVES 4

I N G R E D I E N T S

basic tomato sauce (see page 5)

8 oz/225 g fresh or dried green tagliatelle

fresh basil leaves, to garnish

C H I C K E N   S A U C E

4 tbsp unsalted butter

14 oz/400 g skinless, boneless chicken breast portions, thinly sliced

¾ cup blanched almonds

1¼ cups heavy cream

salt and pepper

1 Make the tomato sauce, set aside, and keep warm.

2 To make the chicken sauce, melt the butter in a large, heavy skillet over medium heat. Add the chicken pieces and almonds and cook, stirring frequently, for about 5–6 minutes, until the chicken is cooked through.

3 Meanwhile, pour the cream into a small pan, set over low heat, and bring to a boil. Boil for about 10 minutes, until reduced by almost half. Pour the cream over the chicken and almonds, stir well, and season with salt and pepper to taste. Remove the pan from the heat, set aside, and keep warm.

4 Bring a large pan of lightly salted water to a boil. Add the pasta, bring back to a boil, and cook until tender but still firm to the bite. Fresh tagliatelle will take 2–3 minutes and dried pasta will take 8–10 minutes, timed from when the water returns to a boil. Drain, then return to the pan, cover, and keep warm.

5 When ready to serve, turn the pasta into a warmed serving dish and spoon the tomato sauce over it. Spoon the chicken and cream into the center, sprinkle with the basil leaves, and serve.

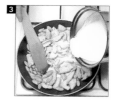